"<u>BROKEN DOLL</u>"

Poetry And Artwork
From The Mental Hospital

Michelle Torez

"BROKEN DOLL"

Michelle Torez

Copyright

Originally Published in 2015, this edition 2018
Copyright © Michelle Torez

Michelle Torez asserts the moral right under the Copyright, Designs and Patents Act 1988 to be identified as the author of this work.

British Library C.I.P.

A CIP catalogue record for this title is available from the British Library.

About The Author Michelle Torez

Michelle Proby was born in October 1994 in Hull, Yorkshire, England. She was brought up by her lone father due to her mother having serious mental health problems. At the tender age of twelve following a mental breakdown, Michelle took a knife to her secondary school and waited outside, ready to threaten people with it. She was subsequently arrested, charged with 'possession of an offensive weapon' and subjected to a section 37 hospital order. She was kept locked up for 5 years in 'Roycroft Clinic', a scandal infested unit in Newcastle Upon Tyne where she was subjected to mental and sexual abuse. This unit is where Michelle wrote most of these poems. Luckily many staff got sacked for child abuse and inappropriate behaviour. The newspaper articles on this are still available to read. Type 'Roycroft Clinic Newcastle' into google if you'd like to read about this. After this unit Michelle was sent around the country like a parcel for a further three years until she was finally released from the 'system'. Many professionals can't understand why Michelle was locked up for so long and have agreed with Michelle's view that it was ridiculously unfair and counterproductive as it has damaged Michelle's ability to develop socially and emotionally. In total, Michelle served   8 years locked up in secure services which is the equivalent of getting a 16 year sentence in prison. People do less for armed robbery or even rape. Due to having this conviction and other mentalhealth related convictions, Michelle has been unable to gain employment and is banned for life for most jobs. The uk mentalhealth system is an uncaring one that criminalizes people far too young. Michelle has been given various mentalhealth diagnoses including Borderline Personality Disorder, Post Traumatic Stress Disorder, Depression & Aspergers Syndrome (a form of Autism)

Michelle currently lives in Leeds, and is studying for a BA (Hons) in English Literature & Creative Writing with The Open University. She is working on new titles and continues to campaign for better mental health services.

Thanks

I give thanks to all of my fans out there that have been liking and buying my work! You have kept me going!

Never Give Up

Thank you for picking up this book. I hope that these poems inspire you. Writing is my life. It is my way of coping with the difficult times that life throws at you. It's my way of turning my experiences into a product for people to keep, hold in their hands and cherish. During my awful time of being locked up in psychiatric units, writing was my only escape from the horrors going on around me. The poems in this book were written mostly whilst I was locked in my cell like room in 'Roycroft Clinic' in Newcastle, a place where over seven members of staff got sacked for child abuse. To anyone that has suffered or is suffering abuse, isolation, depression, I hope that these poems find a place in your mind and I hope that they can help in some way. Through rock bottom helplessness these poems have pulled me through. You can get through too!

I need to give out the message that anything is possible in this world, it really is. Don't let the evil of the world suck you in or drag you down. Be you. Be free. Chase your dreams, not other people's approval.

"Never Give Up"

Michelle

Broken Doll

My life was so delicate
until a single, well-thrown stone broke it,
now my life is desecrated
parts scattered around, some missing,
my life now a broken doll
and now the strings of evil control it.

My life was an antique
but an old, heartless thief stole it,
now I face the mirror
my limp limbs and frail skin,
reflecting in the light
my impurities uncovered,
now *they* control me.
I'm a broken doll
a muse,
a toy to use,
break,
then blame.

Original paintings by Michelle Torez

Original painting by Michelle Torez

Original pen ink drawing by Michelle Torez

Original pencil drawing by Michelle Torez

<u>Cigarette Butts</u>

Cigarette butts are now my fascination
it's the irreversible effect,
life then death
a bit like torture
it goes on, then it goes out
but it cannot be forgotten
the change is irreversible.
I like the way they are pushed, shoved,
squashed into little holes
forced into funny positions
forgotten about straight away.

Cigarette butts are now my fascination
it's the irreversible effect,
light on, light out
like a light to heaven glowing
crying out to be seen
but no,
its used and abused
like one train of thought,
choked on daily
sucking the life out of it.
I like the way the foot drags
upon the stone floor
putting the butt out with no, no effort
like torture it goes on, then it goes out
but it cannot be forgotten.

A Spider

I sit alone and watch a small spider
spin webs of security without thought,
without any malice or bad intention it waits
until a fly gets inevitably caught.
Then, it eats the fly slowly, mindfully
until the small piece of protein is gone,
it then returns to fixing its web again
without any intruding thought of right or wrong.
It appears through cracks and openings
without meaning to cause a fright,
to the pale white person seeing eight spread legs
reflecting in beautiful light,
it has no concept of love or hate
a bit like me, it just wanders aimlessly, unaware, innocent
hoping its web will catch its bait.
I do not have eight legs, but my mind is like a spider
wandering from corner to corner, every dusty place,
now inhabited by cobwebs and dead flies
like my own abandoned living space.
I am not a bad person, honest, please hear
please don't cast me aside with derision,
or squash me with your size
I'm just a small, small spider,
through my small, small eyes.

<u>This Society</u>

The car fumes clog up my nose
with a strong stench of denial, hate,
the emotions that are drawn into us all
so slowly, we can do nothing but wait.

I look through the dirty window
several cobwebs and several flies,
hundreds of people waiting for soup
before the electric cooker dies.

This society is fading away
so slowly, bricks fall to the floor,
soon this demonic society will
take my shoes, my feet, my door.

And then I'll be nothing again
just a number on a plain white page,
my mouth will be sewed shut
so I can't fight against the minimum wage.

These jeans I wear with pride
are mine by bleeding hands, so small,
at night the innocent cries haunt me
as so slowly, the bricks will fall.

This society is fading away
only the strong and heartless will remain,
rejoicing in the spotlight of evil,
rejoicing in the hands of the insane.

Enter Myself

I want to enter myself
I want to dig deep below the surface of my skin,
putting my fingers into the bloody pool
is how I want my purification to begin.

I want to walk inside myself
I want to spray graffiti along the subways of my brain,
these long, winding roads to nothing
have rendered me insane.

I want to swim inside myself
I want to feel the thickness of my blood,
the weight of it, the pull of it, weigh me down
in this self-made androgynous mess
it is time for me to drown.

24/8/10

<u>Take This Woman From Me</u>

Take this woman from me
she is lost in the wrong place,
she has only masculine features
and stubble growing on her face.
Take a knife to these breasts
useless pieces of fatty flesh,
replace them with a defined six-pack
only *then* can you watch me undress.

The man I am inside cries everyday
because outside he can never be seen,
no matter how hard I wash and scrub
he never ever feels clean.

Take this woman from me
she is crying, waiting to go home,
stop creating mounds on my skin
and fucking leave me alone.
Cut my clitoris off, it feels good
but it really shouldn't be there,
I stare into the clean, clean mirror
and cry as I mutter a prayer.

2010

Original pencil drawing by Michelle Torez

Original pencil drawing by Michelle Torez

Original pencil drawing by Michelle Torez

Leave My Bed Untidy

When I die, leave my bed untidy
just like my mind.
Some type of art, my mind was a special piece,
but don't exhibit it in The South Bank Show.
Tell my aggressors that I still hate them, and always will
and tell the people that I love, I still love them and I always
will.

When I die, leave my bed untidy
just like my mind.
Leave the bittersweet taste of anger in your mouth
when you think of me,
that's what I had to taste every time I looked into her eyes.

When I die,
just let me die.
Don't make a big scene out of it, banners and flags and
decorations.
Don't sing lines from the bible,
or dress people up to impress
don't make my funeral a special day,
just put me in the ground and cover me with dirt.

When I die, leave my bed untidy
just like my mind.

Surveillance

Words don't hurt me like they used to
they bounce off me gently, skip lightly along my surface,
they cease to provoke me, anger me and upset me
I'm no longer a public mirror to look into.

Sometimes it feels like my life is still under 24 hour
surveillance
every blink, breath, whisper, caught and recorded, kept away,
to stare at daily and pick at, deciphering every meaning to
every word I say.

Every day the lens is cleaned and checked for damage
every tape is repeatedly played,
checking vigorously for evidence of a crime,
a crime that I never committed, except being a victim to time.

Paranoia

There is so much anger in the world at the moment.
Through every gap in conversation
we learn that the world is closing in on us
inch by inch.
Behind closed doors meetings are going on
talking about weapons,
mass destruction
through every smile we can see cracks, lies,
"The deceitful one"
we are all becoming paranoid of each other
yet, we are all inseparable from each other,
we will drink from each other's well
yet, we want to poison it,
we all live in a small space
yet we want to make it smaller
burn it down
        down
           down.

Evil Monster

How did the soul become converted?
the goodness suddenly disappeared into evil leaving no trace
of it behind,
it seemed that the curtains of truth were shut and jammed
and the vision of happiness blind.

The soul unraveled itself to be a long dirty carpet of sin
but we bow down to the remembrance of the carpet,
the stains of blood, grief and loss still remain
embedded within us all, but we bow down to this carpet.

The smiles emerged when the dirty wrists were cut
even the swords seemed to look satisfied and pleasured,
it seemed that they all had become evil monsters
the babies we had all once treasured.

How did the soul become converted?
the stench of derision and hate sprayed on us like the smell of
burning skin, the fire that rids us of all our enemies
and purifies us all within.

We wash our clothes in the blood of our enemies
even the smell of it seems to smell nicer on our clothes
as if it's meant to be there,
we cut the wrists of the happier people
but we don't really care.

The path of our long winding life is coming to a sudden end
we turned in our weapons of luxury and asked for a pen and
paper to write,
to write the words of raw emotion that led us to our
conversion

the sentences that string together the remembrance of
unhelpful devotion, we turned in our weapons of luxury.

How did the soul become converted?
the goodness suddenly disappeared into evil leaving no trace
of it behind,
it seemed that the curtains of truth were shut and jammed
and the vision of happiness blind.

"CONFUSED" Original pencil drawing by Michelle Torez

<u>Living Gallery</u>

I want my skin to be a living canvas
for you to carefully work on and create,
turn my body into a walking gallery
beautiful ink formations of love and hate.

I crave the needle of ink to pierce
my plain, boring skin to reenergize it, make pure,
make my skin a growing, evolving palette of colours
look at me, look at me, look at me
I'm a passionate, desperate art whore.

January 2013

<u>My Tattoo</u>

"Never give up" are the three words tattooed delicately on my
wrist, they once served a purpose;
they helped motivate me, helped me confront my fears,
but now they are just ink formed letters spread across an
aching, tearing canvas
a dirty stain unable to wipe off, constantly there, like my tears.

17.4.13

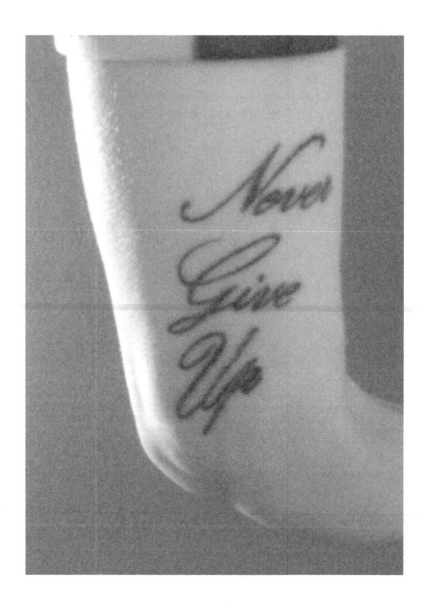

The Nest Is Empty

I watch as hungry chicks swallow the food caring mother
brought for them,
I notice how she watches happily as they gobble it down, then
I sigh,
all I have is a woman that opened her legs and gave birth to
me in a hospital room,
she wasn't there to take away my hunger, make me feel loved,
soothe midnight cries.

She simply cleared off, escaped from my life at only a few
days old, so I was raised by my father, but then taken away by
services gone control mad,
who'd rather try and diagnose me and tick boxes
than let me have a childhood with a caring dad.

I glance at the nest, the chicks are chirping, happy, playing
with mum
so I put on my headphones and listen to some angry, brooding
song,
the nest is empty for me
I find myself being jealous even of nature, since I don't know
where I belong.

I Can Hear The Voices Of My Friends

I can hear the voices of my friends, they whisper me to sleep
as in the white heat of anger I weep and I weep,
they tell me to forget, but I could never forget
this room lay empty now, filled only with regret.

I can see my friends outside the window
they don't look at me, they cannot see,
the person they created when they
turned away and forgot about me.

I sit in a cold, cold room alone with nothing
I know this depression booklet won't save,
those condescending, patronizing sentences
will follow me to my grave.

I can hear the voices of my friends, they whisper me to sleep
as in the white heat of anger
I weep
and I weep.

Pay As You Go Friends (Rap)

All of my life
my so-called "friends" I thought were close
couldn't have been any more distant
I was so transparent, like a ghost,
I was daft not to notice, that they were frauds in disguise
liars looked into my eyes and told a thousand fucking lies,
if I didn't give them money they simply vanished in a dash
they wanted to either trick me, bed me or simply wanted cash,
I refer to these people as "pay as you go friends"
just like a mobile, you need to feed them cash or your
connection quickly ends.

Friendship, A Necessary Pain

Friendship is a necessary pain, a necessary torture,
it's what Humans need to experience in order to grow
stronger,
wiser,
less desperate,
having our hopes and wishes cherished like a new born baby
then murdered, one stab to the heart, it's the start
of a new transformation in being Human,
learning that not every living person gives a shit
but will suck up every one of your last pennies,
until you can't even afford food to live
these once called "friends" will humiliate you,
sit you down on your knees to worship foreign gods
they will strip you of your dignity,
then, when the fad is over
when it's not "cool" anymore,
they will come knocking at around midnight
just about sober,
holding a symbol of peace
be it a flower, or a friendship bracelet
and, foolishly, you will take it,
believing that they have learnt
believing that they have moved on,
but this is the nature of being Human
not knowing where our heart should belong.

12.2.12

A Mistake

A biro pen leak, staining your jean pocket
a relationship that has run its course and is now ready to end,
ink leaking down, seeping through your pocket lining
the guilt of the mistake and how it's hurting a friend.

Washing machine and its partner washing tablet
work well together you say, they can *only* work *when
together*, *dependent* on each other is the truth,
when trying to remove the awkward ink stain
when trying to correct the mistake of a confused youth.

February 2015

This Must Be Depression

I often sit, head in hands, facing the stone grey carpet for hours,
when people come to me and speak I just cannot find the words to reply,
people mutter to themselves quietly and then quickly shuffle away
"This must be depression" the Dr says. Black suit, grey tie.

When I awake from sleep I feel no emotion
some people say that I am ungrateful for not valuing my being,
I never said that I didn't value it; people put words into my mouth,
it just becomes monotonous sometimes, opening eyes, breathing, seeing.

I am often visited by a psychiatrist, a shrink, a waste of time
who asks me question after question as if interrogating an alien species locked in a cage,
How is your sleeping pattern?
What have you been eating?
How are you feeling?
That on its own is enough to drive the saints into a frenzied rage.

Assessment number eleven.
Questions answered, I diverted my eyes to the stone grey carpet like I do, the Dr asked me if I wanted a tea or coffee so I answered politely "no thank you" and I sighed,
it wasn't because I was depressed, I simply did not fancy one,
I had just drunk a bottle of pepsi.
"This must be depression" he says. Black suit, grey tie.

2013

No Interpreter

Visualize everything that makes you who you are
visualize everything that makes your life worth living,
then throw it into the fire, watch as your happiness dissolves
into the flames of raw life,
death can make you do this to yourself.
Streams of tears. A razor sharp knife.

I am living in a world that's as foreign to me now as when I
was born, no words I speak make sense, no interpreter could
interpret the language of grief that I speak.
Watch my tongue flick like a snake, watch my mouth twist
and turn.
Visualize everything you've ever wanted then sit back and
just let it burn.

2014

I Will Stand In Line

I cannot see the future
or walk across treacherous seas,
but I can end madness with silence
while I beg for peace on my knees.
I cannot predict into space
or explore the ocean's blue,
but I can prepare my aching heart
for a remembrance of you.

I will stand in line, hand over my heart,
and worship your gods like everyone else,
I will stand in line and worship your gods
but it doesn't mean I believe in them.

I am not prepared to cross out stars
by worshipping such ill-gotten names,
the picture in the light
is the candle sparking flames.
I do not want to ruin my life
or reduce you to producing tears,
but all I want is to go home
I need not face my fears.

I will stand in line, hand over my heart
and worship your gods like everyone else,
I will stand in line and worship your gods
but it doesn't mean I believe in them.

To Watch The Leaves Fall

I don't want to watch the leaves fall
time and time again,
littering the floor with innocence
I can only stare in pain
because I cannot go outside and feel the harsh wind that blew
them
against my skin, beneath the rain.

September 2011

Hell

I have been through the depths of hell and back
more than once I have looked the devil in the eyes,
for years the sound of jolly laughter and conversation
was replaced by evil taunts and nightmarish cries.

Every day I awoke in a cold sweat, eyes red with over rubbing
thoughts of suicide prominent in my aching, tortured mind,
every waking second breathing and seeing was torture, abuse
the demon's cruel remarks increasing
my self-esteem becoming a slow grind.

Dying bodies hung from fish hooks, bleeding
dripping down the long, winding corridors of evil, of hatred,
of sin, every person a twisted demon only alive to hurt me
I tried many times,
an old, dirty razor against my clean, soft skin,
wrists cut, blood spraying from my open veins, yet I was still
alive,
never could I win, never could I escape
in an existence of torture and lies.

The devil stared at me, large, menacing, squinting eyes up
close
focusing into mine,
words becoming slow and slurry I couldn't listen, I'm sure
I had died.
For minutes, hours, days, I was catatonic, frozen solid, frozen
still, the sight of seeing what humanity had become sickened
made me confused, made me mentally ill.

Every night now I clean my hands, wash them with soap.
I have been through the depths of hell and back
more than once I have looked the devil in the eyes,
for years the sound of jolly laughter and conversation
was replaced by evil taunts and nightmarish cries.

Death was all around me, in every corner and every crevice
lay disemboweled bodies, fractured skulls, amputated limbs
and tongues,
tongues that were used to spread the word of love and peace
from the mind of a kind human being, fresh oxygen from
clean lungs.

Controlled By The Devil (Rap)

I have been through the depths of hell and back so, so many
times that I feel like I must belong there, oh well
or maybe God will banish me there, I can't tell,
I've looked the devil in the eyes
I've listened to evil taunts and haunting cries,
everyday, I'm hearing the same old sad news
people cry out for help but society bloody refuse,
I'm used to this, this awful world, this dark, dark place
where people are still shallow, they'll judge your sexuality or
your race,
people would rather shoot a gun then hold a strangers hand
people cause bloodbaths for a small piece of land,
Oh my god! how low can people get!
as if being cruel and racist was what God wanted
do humans forget?
that it was a human being that gave birth to Jesus Christ
but we still go against him and force others to take lives,
the devil makes me thirst
all the evil things that are probably the worst,
if this is all I'll ever see I'd rather put a gun to my head
I'd love to be found with blood pouring from my head,
thoughts of suicide prominent in my aching, tortured brain
fuck me, I'd rather leave this awful life behind and you can label
me insane, but I'll enjoy every single minute of pain.

After all my effort and everything I've done
I just don't seem to belong,
It feels like the devil is controlling everything I do and say
I've been through the depths of hell and back so, so many times
hopefully one day I'll be asked to stay.

A single red rose on the windowsill
overlooking a garden that's filled
with weeds and neglect, there's little respect
for things that have past their time,
a lot like mine, I feel like I had my time to shine and now its
passed
withered away,
it feels like nobody gives a damn about what I've got to say
I feel like the world has turned away and abandoned me,
left me screaming so loud in a church with no air
silently choking off the bad energy left, its silent you see
I hate myself and everything I now feel,
this mindset I thought only of fantasy has turned out to be oh so
real,
this evil presence surrounds me 360 through the lightest of night
and the darkest of day,
converting the positive energy I have into negativity
all my hope leaking away,
I should have expected this I guess, growing up in such an angry,
violent world that the devil would prey on innocent me
caring girl
angry world!

After all my effort and everything I've done
I just don't seem to belong,
it feels like the devil is controlling everything I do and say
I've been through the depths of hell and back so, so many times
hopefully one day I'll be asked to stay.

<u>Getting Worse</u>

Writing profound lines of poetry that provoke, anger upset,
used to be my talent, my pride, a seed that I watered everyday,
but now my words have no impact, people became bored,
accustomed to my style, here I am, reading other people's
work jealous, clutching a blunt pencil in denial.

Helping words glide smoothly and naturally across the page
finding their own place, used to be my pastime of pleasure,
and a skill that I got both enjoyment and money from
but these past few months have dragged by,
not having my own voice on the page hurts me
every time I try to write something unique, something special,
I criticize myself, tell myself it's wrong.

I'm steadily getting worse and there's little I can do
my brain is slowly fading away,
every wire and connection tangled, tied,
I am proud that I am going to make it as a famous poet one
day, despite all of this
but I'm not so proud that I'm trying to believe a lie.

17.9.13

Blood Of The Ink

I would like my pen to reap vengeance
I want the sharp nib to cut across your skin, causing pain,
each droplet of blood, now an indelible ink
that will hopefully induce such shame.

I want each word to be finished for you
I want your sentences stolen, copyright,
I want you to whisper my name in white anger
through the midst of every night.

I want to tattoo across your naked body
I want my ink to flow through your bloodstream,
the ink will soak up your blood
and my ink will be in your blood, my dream.

August 2011

The Hourglass Is About To Shatter

The hourglass is about to shatter
I can feel it, the tension in the air,
like the silence before the big kill
the fox prying down on the hare.

The glass is about to cut deep
I can almost feel it, trickling down, the blood,
the nauseous, faint feeling of blood loss
the result of never being understood.

The time is about to run out.
Yes! I can see it coming, my biggest comfort, the thought of
achieving suicide,
maybe it wouldn't have resorted to this, this desperation
if you'd have stopped when tears were in my eyes.

3/9/12

Dirty Razor (Rap)

I stare at my blurry wrists through tired, weary eyes
and I smile, in a little while I'll be dead,
suicide equals happiness buzzing around my head
I can't take the monotony anymore, my air is becoming stale
every time I expect to succeed in life, society causes me to
fail, it's fucking sick
the lengths that some people will go to cause other people
pain
mental torture techniques have been practiced on me over and
over again,
they can't stop it
they're addicted,
I'm a prisoner
I'm convicted,
I don't deserve a fresh start in life
so I'm using this razorblade against my throat, a new life.

Searching for the best place for the incision,
this pain will bring no tears.
No, no tears will come from these overused eyes
only derision, people never wanted to help me succeed
people only wanted to laugh watching me fall,
so I'm going to kill myself, happiness equals suicide
you'll be too late when you open the door.

Cutting

Cuts through flesh with ease does a sharp knife
and often the scars will remain forever,
it's simply the science of life
the visual reminder that every Human being is born with the
ability to endure trauma, grief, survive through mental pain,
because after the bleeding of the soul has stopped
a Human will often get up and start again.
These self-created scars should only be worn with a sense of
pride,
no need to feel guilty over doing something that simply
soothed the pain inside,
the Human mind is strong, we will always adapt, find new
ways of coping, ways to survive as our lives progress on
so who the fuck are we to dictate to others that cutting
yourself is wrong?

December 2014

<u>Music Saved My life</u>

I put on my headphones and close my eyes;
music is the reason why I'm still standing here today.
Music is the reason why I can breathe, it takes the pain away.
Listening to the way people string together their words cuts
deep, but it feels so good, it feels so close to me.
Music helps me remember the days and months of happiness
when I was free.
Music has stopped me from cutting through the main vein and
opening the massive void of pain.
Music has given me the strength to put the razor down and
live for another day again.
Music has stopped my fists from bruising innocent bodies in a
frenzied rage.
Music has given me something to focus on whilst locked up in
this hamster cage.
I'm in love with music, music is my only wife.
Thank you music.
Music saved my life.

2010

Let Down

As a kid, I was always aspiring to mingle with the big crowds, the "cool" ones but, somehow, it just didn't happen, I wasn't the right piece for their puzzle it seems,
I was silently deafened by their unheard taunts and selfish laughter, sitting alone
I was muzzled with stinging tears and fading dreams.

Eight years later and I'm still aspiring to fulfil my dream, bestsellers on the shelves,
but sadly my talent is fading away, my gift is floating right pass my clouded eyes,
I'm still trapped tight in this ruthless system I refuse to call my home let down again as usual by awful lies.

2013

The Game

This system was my saviour
it protected me from my inner self,
it cushioned me when I fell
as I became an initial on a shelf.

It helped me grow small wings
to use to search for a new nest,
but I'd become too institutionalized
so I decided to stay with the rest.

This system slowly swallowed me
with kindness, with smothering, with hope,
as it watched me slide up and down
on the negativity slope.

This system washed my wounds
with a special bacterial solution,
it made me wear a mask
to ward off visual pollution.

This system made me happy sometimes
but
this, this system
made me cry
too much.

This system produced excitement
through new curves, new faces, new eyes,
but I became a slave to my own emotions
trapped in a building of a million lies.

The Culprit Of The Crime

I was run over by truth the other day
it didn't hurt much, a few bruises was all that I obtained,
truth asked me to consider going down a different street from
now on but I quickly shook my head and told truth was to
blame.

I slept a deep sleep that night for a change
but when I woke up I was overcome by guilt and pain,
the alarm clock screamed at me to get up, face my fear
but I couldn't, I rolled over, a coward, yet again.

The next day I was awoken by a loud knocking at my door
I knew who it was, it was the police, and they had found the
culprit of the crime,
so I begged and pleaded my innocence with a smug grin on
my face
because after all, to be honest, I enjoy it, handcuff time.

22.3.14

<u>Standing On The Top Step</u>

I now own the house, its mine
every inch of wallpaper, I've carefully designed,
but, although this may be true,
I produce a false smile at the moment because I have no one
to look up to.

My idols and heroes died or became too old
I've been left in this world with advice and instructions only
half-told,
I admire my effort into getting this far, despite the strife
but I feel so overwhelmed with options, I'm not enjoying my
life.

Even though freedom has been given to me after eight long,
painful years,
all those years I spent craving freedom I was wasting my time,
it becomes your worst enemy when your depressed, wanting
to cut away the pain,
I've even considered doing crimes, so I can feel the comfort
of the routine again.

Freedom has become my worst enemy now, such a shame
because I'm standing on top of the stairs to my own house
feeling lower then when I didn't have any freedom at all to
my name,
locked away, at least I had the staff to point a finger at, shout
at and blame
now all I have the motivation to do is sleep, eat, cry and
repeat,
it's hard when your no longer labelled as insane.

<u>Hide</u>

I take the clock from the wall
this item doesn't do me any good,
it constantly reminds me
of the time spent using words I never understood.

I take the tv from its stand
this item, such a waste of time,
the people so beautiful in full colour
but just never will be mine.

I take out the sofas and chairs
comfort, well, it's just not on my side,
when all I can do is sit in this chair
feeling I need a corner, a crevice, to hide.

22.10.11

In The Life Of...

If you could sample a day in the life of me you would not be
able to share your experience;
Your mouth would close and your throat would tighten.
Your hands would seize up and stick next to your body in
comfort.
Your eyelids would permanently close, hiding your delicate
eyes from the frightening reality of my life, your mind's way
of trying to escape.
You would be in constant darkness, like in a coffin.
Your body would prefer it.

Silence

The silence hits me hard
like a brick to a double glazed window,
it shatters the protective layers.
My scarred face reflecting
in its many shards, it reminds me that I'm…
a burst balloon, a hungry vulture feeding,
a torn bed sheet, maggots on a rotting corpse.
Never liked by society
Never was
Never will be.

<u>Light</u>

Light has become my worst enemy
it burns my sensitive eyes,
it reveals to me the world that caused me so much pain,
so much despair,
I am now choosing to continue my being in darkness,
food and water are the necessities,
I want nothing more to be there,
the rest are simply reminders, painful to be around
in my tomb I will die in, happily bone bare.

Questions (Too Many)

Wipe off the blood from your cheek
is it the sweetness of death, you seek?
beyond this shadow of woven skies
dwells a pair of beautiful eyes.

Do I like you?
I ponder in my dreams,
Do I need to?
Did I ever like you at all?
Or was it just the hate that made me fall?

Wipe off the blood from your face
I'll leave you hungry, without a trace,
beyond this world of me and you
is a washed out face to guide me through.

Do I like you?
I ponder in my dreams,
Do I need to?
Did I ever like you at all?
Or was it just the hate that made me fall?

December 2006

<u>Tired</u>

Why are the buildings all so black?
Why are the people all so grey?
Why does my mind erase
the most important thing to say?

Is it because I am tired?
tired of playing this game
mess around with people's emotions,
then sit and hide in shame.
Yes, it's because I am tired
the puzzle now all into one,
I sit and rot in this human blackhole
somewhere that I belong.

Why are the words so hurtful
Why is your smile so wide?
Why do I look back in anger, those times
all I did was try.

Yes, it is because I am tired
the puzzle now all into one,
I sit and rot in this human blackhole
"NHS"
somewhere I belong.

11.8.09

Woman For Sale

In the shining shop window, full of neon lights
"WOMAN FOR SALE"
there she stands, trying to smile
half-dressed,
her legs on display for people to gawk at
she aint impressed,
her tight fitting clothes accentuating every curve
her eyes a bluish blur
wandering from the floor to the sky,
as she wonders why the people of today
don't care if they make her cry.

24.8.11

Currency, The Power

I hold a ten pound note between my long, slender fingers and
I sigh, this small piece of paper is life or death for some
people but, within a blink of an eye,
some people can't help themselves, they've spent it-
gone.
This is an artefact of humankind
this is how we live, this is why we die,
it's so surreal how a little piece of paper can change lives.
I put a lighter to it, then strike,
as I watch it burn I can see it all;
coffins being lowered
smiles being wiped away
starving people feasting on crumbs
frightened prostitute.
And then, when there's nothing left
I smile a vain, pretentious kind of smile,
I've burnt a piece of paper again
I've spent it too quick,
I've killed thousands of people again
between my vain, bony, fingers.

Every Blink Is A Second In Time

Every blink is a second in time, never to return
our eyes are like cameras, taking photos of our life,
click click clicking
some of these photos are pretty and airbrushed
but on some of them the ink has run, leaving them blurred,
colours merged into one,
through my young years I will cherish this camera
because, in a few clicks, there will be none.

Every Little Thing

Every little thing makes up the world, the lights, but also the darks.

Every streetlamp makes a completed street.

Every street makes a completed city.

Everything has its place, like a jigsaw, each piece slots in.
I must not lose sight of this, the bigger picture.

Every teardrop saved over years could make a lake, a river, an ocean.

Every time I cry and feel that I cannot go on anymore, I must remember that there is so much beauty in this life.

Every flower on a tree, every creature, every flowing stream, every setting sun.

These things are all free and, no matter where I am, I will always be able to cherish these things.

You see, every little thing makes up the world, but, it had to start from something. Something so small.

Kalahari

The sun's honey rays are shining onto the grass and are
reflecting off trees
dying the ground a golden colour as the wildlife sleep and I'm
taking pictures on my knees,
wind bustling through leaves gently as if to say "*I have no
rush to go anywhere* "
I outstretched my arms in the Kalahari and thanked God, said
a prayer.

Instead of a lightbulb in a dull room
the sun's honey rays are shining onto the grass and are
reflecting off trees,
dying the ground a golden colour as the wildlife sleep
and I'm taking pictures on my knees,
instead of cars and footsteps I can hear the birds singing
and the wind bustling through leaves,
it's too expensive for many Humans to ever come here
but just in case, no technology or houses please.
Stop.
Take a minute in silence while nature grieves.

January 2015

Secretly Looking At Porn

I take it, fold it up or download it
and then hide it, stash it away like a rabbit in their little den,
like a druggie or alcoholic trying to hide their habit
people come, fail to find it, then it resurfaces again.
Like a shot directly into the main vein
these images stimulate,
cause a quickness in my heartbeat
and cause my temperature to rise,
I'm secretly looking at porn, it's against all the hospital rules
and to make it worse, it's the lesbian sort,
the stuff many people despise.

It Pours

It pours from me, the desperation
like water glides down a flowing stream,
the urge to fill up my heart's gaping hole
but at the same time, be kept clean.

With a friend, I will laugh and smile
suppressing my inner torment and distress,
the urge to shout out how I really feel
and not face the consequence,
clean up the social mess.

From a far you may see me as delicate
but please try and not be so naïve,
every time I meet someone I'm starting
plotting new ways to control, new waves to deceive.

19.2.12

Ongoing Commentary

I would love to be your commentator
making comments and remarks about your life,
always honest, some light-hearted, good-natured remarks
some sharp and hurtful, like a knife.

I would like to watch down on you
sleeping peacefully, wrapped, tangled up in your man,
soft, silky pyjamas and him in boxers
but, you see, I've never really been a fan of fake tan.

I would love to talk about your body
commenting on every accentuated curve,
as if you were an animal on a documentary
I'd talk along to every prance and swerve.

I would love to be your commentator
making comments about how I want to be with you,
how I want to caress your body with love
and make my career, my life, come true.

September 2011

Love Is A Strange Word

Love is a strange word, it's often overused
stuck on too many things like labels
verbally abused.
I guess it's just me that still holds onto the word
cherishes it dearly, like a new-born baby,
uses it when necessary, when absolutely needed
to describe the passion felt dearly within,
for a person who is screaming silently
you see, love is such a strange thing.
It coerces the body into a frenzied state
like a drug addict wanting a fix,
love is something that changes the world
brings light, brings darkness,
brings the one in love a total eclipse.

21.10.11

No Cure

I watch the hospital light flicker
on and off in a continuous rage,
as all I can do is lie here alone
trapped in an NHS sleeping cage.

The doctors and nurses come and go
reviewing my shortening chances of life,
if I can't hear, feel or see my girlfriend Remi
I will sell my body to your knife.

"There is no cure for this"
they tell me smugly everyday,
but I know there is
I'm sure there is,
but they don't seem to hear me any day.
Remi is my medicine
she soothes my burning soul and heart,
she is my only painkiller
I'd rather be dead than have to part.
I cannot overdose on her
she is a needed chemical for my brain,
Dr. I sincerely believe that not seeing her
is making me go insane.

My Ghost Girlfriend

Every night now for the past four years
I've been awoken by my future, skin red by my burning tears,
I hear a loud calling
"Michelle, Michelle its me, I'm here".
I walk down the stairs, every stair creaking with weight
I'm travelling to see her, my girlfriend of future fate.
I walk through the wood of green and warm orange
to feel her fingers slide down my neck,
down my back again
to feel her hot lips press against mine
to feel cared for and loved for once,
but for only a limited amount of time.

Out of the orange burst clearing, I see her ghostly frame rise
floating towards me with clear blue, innocent eyes,
she holds her slender hands out, calling my name
awaiting to soothe me, take away all of my pain,
she puts her arms around me, hot lips against mine
then she whispers in my ear "this is the last time",
she twists and turns her body, my heart pounding like a drum
as we combine together and get lost in beautiful sensual fun,
but as my breasts touch hers, she suddenly fades into the
amber glow of the moonlight,
nothing left, just the t-shirt that she wore, a titanium white
tears come to my eyes, stinging like the sting from an angry
bee
this woman is in love with me, but has not yet really met me,
the truth is that she is just a transparent greyish mass
from a troubled imagination, created to help the pain pass,
before my appetite for love simply drives me insane
and another pretend figure invites me in, yet again.

Original pencil drawing by Michelle Torez

Original pen and pencil drawing by Michelle Torez

A Bearable Place

I can feel the cool air of freedom
through my window
through my hair,
the breeze whispering softly in my ears
telling me it misses me being out there.

I look to the floor and sigh
freedom, something I've craved for many, many years,
it's been the product of my anger
the source of my regret-filled tears,
but now it's something that scares me
fills me up with denial and fear,
the craving of being back to normality
yet, the constant longing for you to be near.

I love you with all of my soul girl
you make the world such a bearable place,
although I may see the same four walls
I get to see your beautifully designed face
with you, I've learned I don't care about where I stay,
because I would always love you
in a golden palace
in a heap of hay.

I love you with such honesty
such raw integrity, straight from my heart,
all I want to do is protect you from evil
but you don't want it
you'd rather me depart.

But, listen, although I craved freedom
for far too long, too many years,
I didn't have the grace of your presence
to suppress my anger, solidify my tears,
I don't care about the future anymore
because everything I've ever dreamed of is in you,
so when I pack my inanimate objects
I won't be packing my heart or soul too,
no, you see everything I've ever needed
was right here, right with you,
so although my physical form may be leaving
I'm leaving my heart and soul right here, right with you.

12.10.11

Her Name Was Not Important

Her blonde hair sat gently on her petite shoulders
cushioning her small, delicate, beautiful frame,
her eyes ever changing shades of mystery
unimportant was her name.

She moved with such grace and confidence
I was so attracted; her femininity flowed from her like a stream,
but we only exchanged a few words here and there
name unimportant, she's now labelled only in dream.

I know nothing about her fascinating existence
except from the fact that I loved her from afar, wanted to know more,
but hastily into the world of emptiness and confusion I went
and she double locked her front door.

Her name was not important
I will remember her only from her beautiful smile,
I was so attracted; her femininity flowed from her like a stream
slowly, gently, she evaporated into this massive world
she's now labelled only in dream.

19.1.13

<u>Nicola</u>

I can still feel it through my body,
the painful goodbye handshake
your warmth centered my palm
as blood rushed to my excited heart,
you were once what I needed to survive,
breathe and be contented in this harsh life
now, since we are so distant,
I handshake myself,
with a butcher knife.
I enjoy the feel of it, the blood running down
from open cuts in my hand
pain isn't as strong as love,
but I'm trying my best to cover you up, block you out,
because every time I look in the mirror
or see "Nicola" printed or written down,
I see you elegantly dressed next to the devil, the devil wearing
a crown.

24/6/13

I Only Spoke To You

I only spoke to you
never did our hands touch,
never did our lips meet
the softness of yours against mine
the taste bittersweet.
Never did you give me any indication of an interest, a sexual
tension for me.
A longing.
A wanting.
Never.
I only spoke to you.

I only spoke to you
and, never did our words mean anything
apart from time passing
and idle chatting,
I only spoke to you about the world
never about the importance, you with me,
and do you want to know why?
I knew you didn't care less really.

I only spoke to you
yet, I needed so much more,
you and me snuggled under hot blankets
behind a double-locked door.
But, although I hate it
the thought that your gone,
those words are all I have
of a broken memory,
something wrong.

2011

Cold Dancing

We both knew this moment would arise,
us two the spotlight at the wedding disco
dancing so passionately,
every twist and turn of our limbs symbolising love,
sex even.
But no. Not this time. Not anymore.
I'm staring into your bright green emerald eyes out of guilt
now,
I feel no desire, no wanting, no real intention to be here,
I'm not enjoying your over sexualized salsa
your breasts thrusting embarrassingly near,
you're hot and aroused, your heart is beating,
pounding like a drum,
but I'm afraid the soundtrack to this love story has been
stolen, re-written, re-sung.
I'm not dancing with you anymore; I'm dancing with a cage
a woman that used to bring me love, affection, is now only a
woman withering with age,
you may be hot and flourished, quick stepping, fox-trotting
into the night
but I'm stone cold while dancing with you,
inside this really doesn't feel right.

4/2/13

<u>Only When She's Gone</u>

Only when she's gone
can you fully understand,
how much you really craved it
the warmth of her soft, gentle hands.

Only when she's gone
you can truly realize,
how calm and relaxed you became
looking into her eyes.

Only when she's gone
you can finish the unfinished sentence
with one single word,
and it comes so naturally to you
like a heartbeat,
spread wings of a bird.

Only when she's gone
your heart busts a valve…

Only when she's gone
your eyes stick to the picture frame,
breathing only sporadically
reciting her name again and again.

<u>Personal Coping</u>

Now you're gone all that's left for me is to masturbate
in an empty, lifeless room,
forgotten about
like our unborn baby in your swollen womb,
it's the only thing that is left
to remind me of how it felt, sex with you,
invigorating, exciting, sensual
but none of it mutually true,
you see I was utterly attracted back then
but now the attraction is starting to fade,
as I lay here trying to bring it all back
I lay here drowning in memories,
deep water in which I must wade.

<u>Some Anger</u>

Being kind and caring all the time is beginning to wear me out
I can feel the urge in me to just let the hate pour from me,
scream and shout,
to feed my inner demon, the anger, the lit flame inside
that smolders, craving to be let out and start a fire,
since you cheated on me and lied every time I now open my
mouth I need a spark, some anger
my desire.

Icicles

I always wanted to be close to you
I craved the touch of your fingers against mine,
your eyes a blue sky
a safe haven for me to stay,
but now I can't stand the sight of them
I feel calmer when looking away,
now your fingers feel like icicles
when you touch me,
you freeze me
in one time
in one place
in the captivating memory of when being with you
wasn't being with a disgrace.

25/10/11

Too Late For Love

I tell you everyday that I love you
in my own unique, personal way,
through the subtleties of my body language
through the words, so kind, I will say.
I tell you loud and clear
but you turn an intimidating blind eye,
you reply to my words of affection
with a patronizing kind of sigh.

Even though I know you don't love me
even though I know you don't want me,
even though I know you don't need me
even though I know once you step out of this building I don't
even enter your mind;

I tell you everyday that I love you
but one day I won't say it,
or even mutter it
no worrying over you
I will pretend not to care,
from then on I will continue with my life
pretending you were never there.

November 2011

Broken Doll

My life was so delicate
a single, well-thrown stone broke it,
now my life is desecrated
parts scattered around, some missing,
my life now a broken doll
and now the strings of evil control it.

My life was an antique
but an old, heartless thief stole it,
now I face the mirror
my limp limbs and frail skin,
reflecting in the light
my impurities uncovered,
now *they* control me.
I'm a broken doll
a muse,
a toy to use,
break,
blame.

Thankyou for reading. If you like this title you will most likely enjoy my Youtube channel were I upload regular spokenword poetry, mentalhealth advice videos and alternative rap music.

https://www.youtube.com/michelletorez

Printed in Great Britain
by Amazon

38523397R00047